50 Low-Sodium Snack Idea Recipes for Home

By: Kelly Johnson

Table of Contents

- Sliced cucumbers with hummus
- Greek yogurt with fresh berries
- Air-popped popcorn sprinkled with nutritional yeast
- Rice cakes topped with avocado and cherry tomatoes
- Apple slices with almond butter
- Carrot sticks with tzatziki sauce
- Cottage cheese with pineapple chunks
- Edamame beans sprinkled with sea salt
- Whole grain crackers with low-sodium deli meat
- Trail mix with unsalted nuts and dried fruits
- Celery sticks filled with cream cheese
- Sliced bell peppers dipped in guacamole
- Low-sodium cheese sticks
- Hard-boiled eggs
- Homemade kale chips
- Baked sweet potato fries
- Brown rice cakes with mashed avocado
- Steamed edamame beans sprinkled with sesame seeds
- Cherry tomatoes stuffed with tuna salad
- Greek yogurt parfait with low-sodium granola
- Sliced pear with ricotta cheese
- Roasted chickpeas with garlic and herbs
- Ants on a log (celery sticks with peanut butter and raisins)
- Whole grain toast with mashed banana
- Frozen grapes
- Mini bell peppers filled with hummus
- Cottage cheese with sliced peaches
- Seaweed snacks
- Quinoa salad with cucumber and lemon dressing
- Rice crackers with avocado and smoked salmon
- Beet chips
- Greek yogurt with chia seeds and honey
- Caprese skewers (cherry tomatoes, mozzarella balls, and basil)
- Almond butter and banana roll-ups
- Veggie sushi rolls with low-sodium soy sauce

- Whole grain pretzels with mustard for dipping
- Baked apple chips
- Guacamole with cucumber slices
- Brown rice cakes with almond butter and sliced strawberries
- Greek yogurt dip with fresh vegetables
- Cottage cheese with sliced kiwi
- Veggie sticks with homemade ranch dip
- Peanut butter and jelly on whole grain crackers
- Baked cinnamon apple slices
- Whole grain pita chips with roasted red pepper hummus
- Low-sodium turkey roll-ups with lettuce and mustard
- Mixed nuts (unsalted)
- Rice cakes with mashed avocado and sliced hard-boiled eggs
- Baked carrot fries
- Greek yogurt with mango chunks

Sliced cucumbers with hummus

Ingredients:

- Fresh cucumbers, washed and sliced
- Hummus (store-bought or homemade)

Instructions:

1. Wash the cucumbers thoroughly under cold water to remove any dirt or debris.
2. Slice the cucumbers into rounds or sticks, depending on your preference. You can also peel the cucumbers if desired, although the skin adds extra texture and nutrients.
3. Spoon a dollop of hummus onto a plate or into a small bowl.
4. Arrange the cucumber slices around the hummus for easy dipping.
5. Dip the cucumber slices into the hummus and enjoy!

Tips:

- Choose firm and crisp cucumbers for the best texture.
- Feel free to experiment with different flavors of hummus, such as roasted red pepper, garlic, or spicy hummus.
- Garnish the hummus with a drizzle of olive oil, a sprinkle of paprika, or a few fresh herbs for extra flavor and visual appeal.
- Serve this snack as a light appetizer, midday pick-me-up, or part of a healthy lunch or dinner spread.

Sliced cucumbers with hummus are not only delicious but also a great source of hydration, fiber, and essential vitamins and minerals. Enjoy this nutritious snack anytime for a satisfying and refreshing treat!

Greek yogurt with fresh berries

Ingredients:

- Greek yogurt (plain or flavored)
- Fresh berries (such as strawberries, blueberries, raspberries, or blackberries)
- Optional toppings: honey, granola, chopped nuts, or shredded coconut

Instructions:

1. Start by choosing your favorite type of Greek yogurt. You can use plain Greek yogurt for a tangy flavor or flavored Greek yogurt for added sweetness.
2. Wash the fresh berries thoroughly under cold water and pat them dry with a paper towel. You can use a single type of berry or a mix of different berries for variety.
3. If using strawberries, remove the stems and slice them into smaller pieces.
4. Spoon a serving of Greek yogurt into a bowl or glass.
5. Top the Greek yogurt with a generous portion of fresh berries.
6. If desired, drizzle the yogurt and berries with a little honey for extra sweetness.
7. For added crunch and texture, sprinkle some granola, chopped nuts, or shredded coconut on top.
8. Serve immediately and enjoy your delicious Greek yogurt with fresh berries!

Tips:

- Greek yogurt is rich in protein, calcium, and probiotics, making it a healthy choice for snacks or breakfast.
- Fresh berries are loaded with antioxidants, vitamins, and fiber, making them a nutritious addition to your diet.
- Feel free to customize your yogurt bowl with your favorite toppings, such as seeds, dried fruits, or a sprinkle of cinnamon.
- This snack is also great for meal prep. You can portion out individual servings of Greek yogurt and berries into containers for easy grab-and-go snacks throughout the week.

Greek yogurt with fresh berries is not only delicious but also satisfying and nutritious. It's a versatile snack that's sure to please your taste buds and keep you feeling energized and satisfied.

Air-popped popcorn sprinkled with nutritional yeast

Ingredients:

- 1/4 cup popcorn kernels
- 1-2 tablespoons nutritional yeast
- Salt, to taste (optional)

Instructions:

1. Start by popping the popcorn kernels using an air popper. If you don't have an air popper, you can also pop the kernels in a large pot on the stovetop with a little oil.
2. Once the popcorn is popped, transfer it to a large bowl.
3. Sprinkle the nutritional yeast over the popcorn, using as much or as little as you like depending on your preference.
4. If desired, add a pinch of salt to the popcorn for extra flavor. Keep in mind that nutritional yeast adds a savory, cheesy flavor, so you may not need much additional salt.
5. Toss the popcorn gently to evenly distribute the nutritional yeast and salt.
6. Serve immediately and enjoy your delicious air-popped popcorn sprinkled with nutritional yeast!

Tips:

- Nutritional yeast is a great source of vitamins, minerals, and protein, and it adds a delicious cheesy flavor to popcorn without the need for butter or cheese.
- You can find nutritional yeast at most health food stores or online. Look for it in the bulk section or with other packaged goods.
- Feel free to get creative and add other seasonings to your popcorn, such as garlic powder, onion powder, smoked paprika, or chili powder, for extra flavor.
- Air-popped popcorn is a healthy and low-calorie snack that's high in fiber and whole grains, making it a great choice for satisfying your hunger between meals.

Enjoy your nutritious and delicious air-popped popcorn sprinkled with nutritional yeast as a guilt-free snack anytime you need a crunchy and savory treat!

Rice cakes topped with avocado and cherry tomatoes

Ingredients:

- Rice cakes (choose your favorite variety)
- 1 ripe avocado
- Cherry tomatoes
- Salt and pepper, to taste
- Optional toppings: red pepper flakes, sesame seeds, balsamic glaze, or fresh herbs like basil or cilantro

Instructions:

1. Start by slicing the avocado in half and removing the pit. Scoop out the flesh into a small bowl and mash it with a fork until smooth. Season with salt and pepper to taste.
2. Wash the cherry tomatoes and slice them in half.
3. Place the rice cakes on a serving platter or individual plates.
4. Spread a generous layer of mashed avocado onto each rice cake.
5. Top the avocado layer with halved cherry tomatoes, pressing them gently into the avocado to help them stick.
6. Sprinkle the assembled rice cakes with additional salt and pepper, if desired.
7. If using any optional toppings like red pepper flakes, sesame seeds, or fresh herbs, sprinkle them over the top of the rice cakes.
8. Serve the rice cakes topped with avocado and cherry tomatoes immediately and enjoy!

Tips:

- Choose rice cakes that are sturdy enough to hold the toppings without breaking. You can use plain rice cakes or opt for flavored varieties like multigrain or brown rice for extra flavor and texture.
- Feel free to customize the toppings based on your preferences. You can add sliced cucumbers, radishes, or red onions for extra crunch, or drizzle the rice cakes with balsamic glaze or a squeeze of lemon juice for added flavor.
- These rice cakes make for a versatile snack or light meal. Enjoy them as a quick and easy breakfast, a satisfying afternoon snack, or a light lunch alongside a salad or soup.

These rice cakes topped with avocado and cherry tomatoes are not only delicious but also packed with healthy fats, fiber, vitamins, and minerals. They're perfect for satisfying your hunger and keeping you energized throughout the day!

Apple slices with almond butter

Ingredients:

- 1-2 crisp apples (such as Honeycrisp, Gala, or Fuji)
- Almond butter (or your favorite nut butter)
- Optional toppings: cinnamon, honey, chopped nuts, or shredded coconut

Instructions:

1. Wash the apples thoroughly under cold water and pat them dry with a clean towel.
2. Core the apples and slice them into thin wedges or rounds using a sharp knife or apple slicer. You can leave the skin on for extra fiber and nutrients, or peel the apples if you prefer.
3. Spread a generous amount of almond butter onto each apple slice. You can use smooth or crunchy almond butter, depending on your preference.
4. If desired, sprinkle the almond butter with a pinch of cinnamon for extra flavor. You can also drizzle a little honey over the top for added sweetness.
5. For additional texture and crunch, sprinkle chopped nuts or shredded coconut over the almond butter.
6. Arrange the apple slices with almond butter on a serving platter or plate.
7. Serve immediately and enjoy your delicious apple slices with almond butter!

Tips:

- Choose apples that are firm and crisp for the best texture and flavor. You can use any variety of apple you like, but sweeter varieties like Honeycrisp or Gala pair especially well with almond butter.
- If you're preparing apple slices ahead of time, you can prevent them from browning by soaking them in a mixture of water and lemon juice or tossing them with a little lemon juice before serving.
- Feel free to get creative with your toppings! You can sprinkle the almond butter with chia seeds, hemp seeds, or granola for added nutrition and crunch.
- These apple slices with almond butter make for a satisfying and nutritious snack any time of day. Enjoy them as a quick breakfast, a midday pick-me-up, or a healthy dessert option.

Apple slices with almond butter are not only delicious but also packed with fiber, protein, and healthy fats, making them a nutritious and satisfying snack option that's sure to please your taste buds!

Carrot sticks with tzatziki sauce

Ingredients:

For the Tzatziki Sauce:

- 1 cup Greek yogurt
- 1/2 cucumber, grated and drained
- 1-2 cloves garlic, minced
- 1 tablespoon fresh lemon juice
- 1 tablespoon extra virgin olive oil
- 1 tablespoon chopped fresh dill
- Salt and pepper to taste

For the Carrot Sticks:

- Fresh carrots, washed, peeled, and cut into sticks

Instructions:

1. Prepare the Tzatziki Sauce:

    1. Grate the cucumber using a box grater or food processor. Place the grated cucumber in a fine-mesh sieve or cheesecloth and squeeze out excess moisture.
    2. In a mixing bowl, combine the Greek yogurt, grated and drained cucumber, minced garlic, lemon juice, olive oil, chopped dill, salt, and pepper. Mix until well combined.
    3. Taste the tzatziki sauce and adjust the seasoning as needed. You can add more garlic, lemon juice, or salt according to your preference.
    4. Cover the tzatziki sauce and refrigerate for at least 30 minutes to allow the flavors to meld together.

2. Prepare the Carrot Sticks:

    1. Wash the carrots thoroughly under cold water to remove any dirt or debris.

2. Peel the carrots using a vegetable peeler, if desired.
3. Cut the carrots into sticks, approximately 3-4 inches long and 1/4 inch thick.

3. Serve:

1. Transfer the chilled tzatziki sauce to a serving bowl and place it on a platter.
2. Arrange the carrot sticks around the tzatziki sauce bowl for dipping.
3. Serve immediately and enjoy your delicious carrot sticks with tzatziki sauce!

Tips:

- For a creamier tzatziki sauce, you can use full-fat Greek yogurt. If you prefer a lighter option, you can use low-fat or non-fat Greek yogurt instead.
- Feel free to customize the tzatziki sauce to your taste preferences. You can add finely chopped mint or parsley for additional freshness, or a pinch of paprika for a subtle smoky flavor.
- Carrot sticks with tzatziki sauce make for a healthy and satisfying snack that's perfect for parties, picnics, or as an afternoon snack. They're also a great way to get more vegetables into your diet while enjoying a delicious and creamy dip!

Cottage cheese with pineapple chunks

Ingredients:

- 1 cup of cottage cheese
- 1 cup of fresh pineapple chunks (you can also use canned pineapple chunks, just make sure to drain the juice)
- Optional: a drizzle of honey or a sprinkle of cinnamon for extra flavor

Instructions:

1. If you're using fresh pineapple, start by peeling and cutting it into bite-sized chunks. If you're using canned pineapple, drain the juice from the chunks.
2. Place the cottage cheese in a serving bowl.
3. Add the pineapple chunks on top of the cottage cheese.
4. If desired, drizzle a little honey over the top for added sweetness or sprinkle some cinnamon for extra flavor.
5. Gently mix everything together, being careful not to break up the pineapple too much.
6. Serve immediately and enjoy!

This recipe is versatile, so feel free to adjust the quantities of cottage cheese and pineapple according to your preference. You can also add other fruits or toppings like nuts or seeds for added texture and flavor.

Edamame beans sprinkled with sea salt

Ingredients:

- 1 cup of edamame beans (frozen or fresh)
- Sea salt, to taste

Instructions:

1. If using frozen edamame beans, thaw them by running them under cold water for a few minutes or microwaving them according to the package instructions. If using fresh edamame beans, rinse them thoroughly.
2. Bring a pot of water to a boil and add the edamame beans.
3. Boil the beans for about 5 minutes, or until they are tender. If you prefer a firmer texture, you can boil them for a shorter amount of time.
4. Once the beans are cooked, drain them and rinse them under cold water to stop the cooking process.
5. Pat the edamame beans dry with a clean kitchen towel or paper towel.
6. Sprinkle the beans with sea salt to taste. Be sure to toss them gently to ensure the salt is evenly distributed.
7. Transfer the seasoned edamame beans to a serving dish and enjoy them as a tasty and nutritious snack!

You can also customize this recipe by adding other seasonings such as garlic powder, chili flakes, or sesame seeds for extra flavor. Experiment with different combinations to find your favorite!

Whole grain crackers with low-sodium deli meat

Ingredients:

- Whole grain crackers
- Low-sodium deli meat slices (such as turkey, chicken, or roast beef)
- Optional: mustard or a slice of cheese for added flavor

Instructions:

1. Lay out the whole grain crackers on a plate or serving tray.
2. Place a slice of low-sodium deli meat on each cracker. You can fold or layer the meat slices depending on your preference.
3. If desired, add a small dollop of mustard on top of the deli meat for extra flavor.
4. If you prefer, you can also add a slice of cheese on top of the deli meat.
5. Arrange the prepared crackers with deli meat on a serving platter and serve immediately.

This snack is not only delicious but also provides a good balance of carbohydrates, protein, and fiber from the whole grain crackers and lean protein from the deli meat. It's perfect for a quick and nutritious bite on the go or as a light appetizer for gatherings. Feel free to customize the toppings with your favorite herbs, veggies, or spreads to suit your taste preferences.

Trail mix with unsalted nuts and dried fruits

Ingredients:

- 1 cup unsalted mixed nuts (such as almonds, cashews, walnuts, and peanuts)
- 1 cup dried fruits (such as raisins, cranberries, apricots, and cherries)
- Optional add-ins: dark chocolate chips, pumpkin seeds, sunflower seeds, coconut flakes, whole grain cereal

Instructions:

1. If your nuts are not already unsalted, you can rinse them under cold water and pat them dry with a clean towel to remove excess salt.
2. In a large mixing bowl, combine the unsalted mixed nuts and dried fruits.
3. If you're adding any optional ingredients like chocolate chips or coconut flakes, add them to the bowl as well.
4. Toss the ingredients together until they are evenly distributed.
5. Transfer the trail mix to an airtight container or individual snack bags for easy portioning.
6. Store the trail mix in a cool, dry place for up to several weeks.

This trail mix is perfect for snacking on the go, hiking, or as a topping for yogurt or oatmeal. It's packed with protein, healthy fats, and fiber, making it a satisfying and nutritious option to keep you fueled throughout the day. Feel free to customize the mix by adding your favorite nuts, fruits, and other ingredients to suit your taste preferences and dietary needs.

Celery sticks filled with cream cheese

Ingredients:

- Celery stalks, washed and trimmed
- Cream cheese, softened
- Optional: herbs or seasonings for flavor (such as chopped chives, dill, garlic powder, or black pepper)

Instructions:

1. Wash the celery stalks thoroughly and trim off the ends.
2. In a mixing bowl, combine the softened cream cheese with any desired herbs or seasonings. Mix well until the ingredients are evenly incorporated.
3. Using a knife or small spatula, spread the cream cheese mixture into the hollow part of each celery stalk.
4. Once filled, you can leave the celery sticks whole or cut them into smaller pieces for bite-sized snacks.
5. Arrange the filled celery sticks on a serving platter and serve immediately, or refrigerate them until ready to serve.

These cream cheese-filled celery sticks are not only tasty but also a great way to incorporate more vegetables and calcium-rich dairy into your diet. They make for a refreshing and crunchy snack that's perfect for parties, picnics, or anytime you need a quick bite. Feel free to get creative with the cream cheese filling by adding different herbs, spices, or even chopped nuts for extra flavor and texture.

Sliced bell peppers dipped in guacamole

Ingredients:

- Bell peppers (any color), washed and sliced into strips
- 2 ripe avocados
- 1 lime, juiced
- 1 small tomato, diced
- 1/4 cup red onion, finely chopped
- 1 small jalapeño pepper, seeded and minced (optional, for some heat)
- 2 tablespoons fresh cilantro, chopped
- Salt and pepper to taste

Instructions:

1. Slice the bell peppers into strips and arrange them on a serving platter.
2. Cut the avocados in half, remove the pits, and scoop the flesh into a bowl.
3. Mash the avocados with a fork until smooth or leave it slightly chunky if you prefer.
4. Add lime juice to the mashed avocado and mix well to prevent browning.
5. Stir in the diced tomato, chopped red onion, minced jalapeño (if using), and chopped cilantro. Mix until all ingredients are well combined.
6. Season the guacamole with salt and pepper to taste, adjusting as needed.
7. Transfer the guacamole to a serving bowl and place it in the center of the platter with the sliced bell peppers.
8. Serve immediately and enjoy dipping the bell pepper strips into the guacamole!

This snack is not only delicious but also packed with healthy fats, vitamins, and minerals from the avocado and bell peppers. It's perfect for parties, gatherings, or as a quick and easy snack anytime. Feel free to adjust the ingredients and seasonings according to your taste preferences.

Low-sodium cheese sticks

Ingredients:

- Low-sodium cheese slices or blocks (such as mozzarella or cheddar)
- Optional: whole grain crackers or apple slices for serving

Instructions:

1. Start by selecting low-sodium cheese varieties. Look for options labeled as "low-sodium" or "reduced sodium" at your grocery store. Mozzarella and cheddar are popular choices for cheese sticks.
2. If using cheese slices, cut them into thin strips, about 1/2 inch wide. If using cheese blocks, cut them into rectangular shapes, similar in size to traditional cheese sticks.
3. If desired, you can serve the cheese sticks with whole grain crackers or apple slices for added fiber and flavor.
4. Arrange the cheese sticks on a serving platter or plate.
5. Serve immediately or store them in an airtight container in the refrigerator until ready to eat.

These low-sodium cheese sticks are a great source of protein and calcium, making them a nutritious snack option. They're perfect for packing in lunchboxes, enjoying as an afternoon snack, or as a quick grab-and-go option when you're on the move. Feel free to get creative with your cheese selections and pair them with your favorite accompaniments for a satisfying snack experience.

Hard-boiled eggs

Ingredients:

- Eggs (as many as desired)

Instructions:

1. Place the eggs in a single layer in a saucepan or pot. Make sure they are not stacked on top of each other.
2. Fill the pot with enough water to cover the eggs by about an inch.
3. Place the pot on the stove over high heat and bring the water to a rolling boil.
4. Once the water is boiling, reduce the heat to low and let the eggs simmer for about 10-12 minutes.
5. While the eggs are cooking, prepare a bowl of ice water.
6. After the eggs have cooked for the desired time, use a slotted spoon to transfer them to the bowl of ice water. This helps stop the cooking process and makes the eggs easier to peel.
7. Let the eggs sit in the ice water for about 5 minutes.
8. Once cooled, remove the eggs from the ice water and gently tap them against a hard surface to crack the shell.
9. Peel the shell off each egg under cool running water.
10. Once peeled, the hard-boiled eggs are ready to eat! You can enjoy them whole as a snack, slice them and add them to salads, or mash them with a bit of mayonnaise and mustard for egg salad.

Hard-boiled eggs are a convenient and portable snack that's rich in protein, vitamins, and minerals. They can be stored in the refrigerator for up to one week, making them a great option for meal prep or a quick and healthy snack on the go.

Homemade kale chips

Ingredients:

- 1 bunch of kale
- 1-2 tablespoons of olive oil
- Salt and pepper, to taste
- Optional: garlic powder, paprika, grated Parmesan cheese, nutritional yeast, or other seasonings of your choice

Instructions:

1. Preheat your oven to 300°F (150°C).
2. Wash the kale thoroughly and dry it completely. Use a salad spinner or pat it dry with paper towels.
3. Remove the tough stems from the kale leaves and tear the leaves into bite-sized pieces.
4. In a large bowl, drizzle the kale pieces with olive oil and toss until evenly coated. You want a thin, even layer of oil on each leaf to help them crisp up in the oven.
5. Season the kale with salt and pepper, as well as any additional seasonings you like. Feel free to get creative here!
6. Arrange the kale pieces in a single layer on a baking sheet lined with parchment paper or a silicone baking mat. Make sure the pieces are not overlapping to ensure even baking.
7. Bake the kale chips in the preheated oven for 10-15 minutes, or until they are crisp and slightly browned around the edges. Keep an eye on them towards the end of the cooking time to prevent burning.
8. Once done, remove the kale chips from the oven and let them cool on the baking sheet for a few minutes.
9. Transfer the kale chips to a serving bowl or container and enjoy them immediately! They're best when eaten the same day they're made, but you can store any leftovers in an airtight container at room temperature for a day or two.

Homemade kale chips are a crunchy, flavorful, and guilt-free snack that's packed with vitamins, minerals, and antioxidants. They're a great alternative to store-bought chips and can be customized with your favorite seasonings for endless flavor possibilities.

Baked sweet potato fries

Ingredients:

- 2 large sweet potatoes
- 2 tablespoons olive oil
- 1 teaspoon garlic powder
- 1 teaspoon paprika
- 1/2 teaspoon salt
- 1/4 teaspoon black pepper
- Optional: additional seasonings such as cayenne pepper, rosemary, or thyme

Instructions:

1. Preheat your oven to 425°F (220°C) and line a baking sheet with parchment paper or aluminum foil.
2. Wash the sweet potatoes thoroughly and peel them if desired. Otherwise, scrub them well to remove any dirt.
3. Cut the sweet potatoes into evenly sized fries. Aim for about 1/4 to 1/2 inch thick strips.
4. In a large bowl, toss the sweet potato fries with olive oil until they are evenly coated.
5. In a small bowl, mix together the garlic powder, paprika, salt, and black pepper. You can also add any additional seasonings you like at this point.
6. Sprinkle the seasoning mixture over the sweet potato fries and toss until they are evenly coated.
7. Arrange the seasoned sweet potato fries in a single layer on the prepared baking sheet, making sure they are not overlapping.
8. Bake the sweet potato fries in the preheated oven for 20-25 minutes, flipping them halfway through the cooking time, until they are crispy and golden brown.
9. Once done, remove the sweet potato fries from the oven and let them cool slightly before serving.
10. Enjoy the baked sweet potato fries on their own or with your favorite dipping sauce, such as ketchup, aioli, or sriracha mayo.

These baked sweet potato fries are crispy on the outside and tender on the inside, with just the right amount of seasoning for flavor. They're a healthier alternative to fried potatoes and make a delicious side dish or snack. Feel free to customize the seasonings to suit your taste preferences, and enjoy!

Brown rice cakes with mashed avocado

Ingredients:

- Brown rice cakes
- Ripe avocado
- Salt and pepper, to taste
- Optional toppings: sliced tomato, cucumber, radish, sprouts, or a drizzle of hot sauce

Instructions:

1. Start by slicing a ripe avocado in half and removing the pit. Scoop out the flesh into a bowl.
2. Mash the avocado with a fork until smooth or leave it slightly chunky if you prefer.
3. Season the mashed avocado with salt and pepper to taste, and mix well to combine.
4. Spread a generous amount of mashed avocado onto each brown rice cake.
5. If desired, top the avocado with sliced tomato, cucumber, radish, sprouts, or a drizzle of hot sauce for added flavor and texture.
6. Serve the brown rice cakes with mashed avocado immediately, and enjoy!

This snack is not only tasty but also packed with healthy fats, fiber, and vitamins from the avocado, along with the whole grains in the brown rice cakes. It's a great option for a quick and satisfying snack or light meal, whether you're at home or on the go. Feel free to customize the toppings with your favorite vegetables or seasonings to suit your taste preferences.

Steamed edamame beans sprinkled with sesame seeds

Ingredients:

- Edamame beans (fresh or frozen)
- Sesame seeds
- Salt, to taste (optional)

Instructions:

1. If using frozen edamame beans, thaw them by rinsing them under cold water for a few minutes. If using fresh edamame beans, rinse them thoroughly.
2. In a pot, bring water to a boil. Add a pinch of salt if desired.
3. Once the water is boiling, add the edamame beans to the pot.
4. Boil the edamame beans for about 3-5 minutes, or until they are tender.
5. While the beans are cooking, toast the sesame seeds in a dry skillet over medium heat for 2-3 minutes, or until they are lightly golden brown and fragrant. Stir them frequently to prevent burning.
6. Once the edamame beans are cooked, drain them and transfer them to a serving bowl.
7. Sprinkle the steamed edamame beans with the toasted sesame seeds and a pinch of salt if desired.
8. Toss the beans gently to ensure the sesame seeds are evenly distributed.
9. Serve the steamed edamame beans sprinkled with sesame seeds immediately, and enjoy!

This snack is not only delicious but also packed with protein, fiber, and healthy fats from the edamame beans and sesame seeds. It's perfect for serving as an appetizer, snack, or side dish. Feel free to customize the seasoning by adding other ingredients like soy sauce, garlic, or chili flakes for extra flavor.

Cherry tomatoes stuffed with tuna salad

Ingredients:

- Cherry tomatoes
- 1 can of tuna, drained
- 2-3 tablespoons mayonnaise (or Greek yogurt for a lighter option)
- 1 tablespoon finely chopped red onion
- 1 tablespoon finely chopped celery
- 1 tablespoon chopped fresh parsley or dill
- Salt and pepper, to taste
- Optional: lemon juice, Dijon mustard, or other seasonings of your choice

Instructions:

1. Start by washing the cherry tomatoes and cutting off the tops. You can also slice a small piece off the bottom of each tomato to help them stand upright, if desired.
2. Using a small spoon or melon baller, carefully scoop out the seeds and flesh from each cherry tomato to create a hollow cavity. Be careful not to pierce through the bottom or sides of the tomato.
3. In a mixing bowl, combine the drained tuna, mayonnaise (or Greek yogurt), chopped red onion, chopped celery, and chopped fresh parsley or dill. Mix well to combine.
4. Season the tuna salad mixture with salt and pepper to taste. You can also add a squeeze of lemon juice, a dollop of Dijon mustard, or other seasonings of your choice for added flavor.
5. Once the tuna salad is seasoned to your liking, use a small spoon to fill each hollowed-out cherry tomato with the tuna salad mixture. Fill them until the mixture is slightly mounded on top.
6. Arrange the stuffed cherry tomatoes on a serving platter and garnish with additional chopped parsley or dill, if desired.
7. Serve the stuffed cherry tomatoes with tuna salad immediately, or refrigerate them until ready to serve.

These stuffed cherry tomatoes are not only visually appealing but also packed with protein and flavor. They're perfect for parties, gatherings, or as an elegant appetizer for special occasions. Feel free to customize the tuna salad filling with your favorite ingredients and seasonings to suit your taste preferences. Enjoy!

Greek yogurt parfait with low-sodium granola

Ingredients:

- Greek yogurt (plain or flavored)
- Low-sodium granola
- Fresh berries or sliced fruit (such as strawberries, blueberries, or bananas)
- Optional: honey or maple syrup for sweetness

Instructions:

1. Start by layering a spoonful of Greek yogurt at the bottom of a serving glass or bowl.
2. Add a layer of low-sodium granola on top of the yogurt.
3. Top the granola with a layer of fresh berries or sliced fruit.
4. Repeat the layers until you reach the top of the glass or bowl, finishing with a final layer of yogurt on top.
5. Drizzle a little honey or maple syrup over the yogurt layer for added sweetness, if desired.
6. Optional: garnish with additional fresh berries or a sprinkle of granola on top for extra texture and flavor.
7. Serve the Greek yogurt parfait immediately, or refrigerate it for a few hours to allow the flavors to meld together.

This Greek yogurt parfait with low-sodium granola is not only delicious but also provides a good balance of protein, fiber, vitamins, and minerals. It's a versatile recipe that you can customize with your favorite fruits, nuts, seeds, or other toppings. Enjoy it for breakfast, as a snack, or even as a healthy dessert option!

Sliced pear with ricotta cheese

Ingredients:

- Ripe pear
- Ricotta cheese
- Honey or maple syrup (optional, for drizzling)
- Optional toppings: chopped nuts (such as almonds, walnuts, or pecans), dried fruit (such as cranberries or raisins), cinnamon, or a sprinkle of sea salt

Instructions:

1. Wash the pear thoroughly and slice it into thin slices. You can leave the skin on or peel it according to your preference.
2. Arrange the pear slices on a serving plate or platter.
3. Spoon dollops of ricotta cheese onto the pear slices.
4. Optional: Drizzle a little honey or maple syrup over the pear and ricotta for added sweetness.
5. Optional: Sprinkle chopped nuts, dried fruit, cinnamon, or a pinch of sea salt over the pear and ricotta for additional flavor and texture.
6. Serve the sliced pear with ricotta cheese immediately and enjoy!

This snack is not only delicious but also nutritious, providing a good balance of carbohydrates, protein, and healthy fats. It's perfect for enjoying as a quick and satisfying snack, dessert, or even as a light breakfast option. Feel free to customize the toppings and seasonings according to your taste preferences.

Roasted chickpeas with garlic and herbs

Ingredients:

- 1 can (15 ounces) chickpeas (garbanzo beans), drained and rinsed
- 1 tablespoon olive oil
- 2 cloves garlic, minced
- 1 teaspoon dried herbs (such as rosemary, thyme, oregano, or a combination)
- Salt and pepper, to taste

Instructions:

1. Preheat your oven to 400°F (200°C) and line a baking sheet with parchment paper or aluminum foil.
2. Pat the rinsed chickpeas dry with a clean kitchen towel or paper towels to remove excess moisture.
3. In a mixing bowl, combine the chickpeas with olive oil, minced garlic, dried herbs, salt, and pepper. Toss until the chickpeas are evenly coated.
4. Spread the seasoned chickpeas in a single layer on the prepared baking sheet.
5. Roast the chickpeas in the preheated oven for 20-25 minutes, stirring halfway through, or until they are golden brown and crispy.
6. Once done, remove the roasted chickpeas from the oven and let them cool slightly before serving.
7. Enjoy the roasted chickpeas with garlic and herbs as a crunchy snack on their own, or use them as a topping for salads, soups, or grain bowls.

These roasted chickpeas with garlic and herbs are not only delicious but also packed with protein and fiber, making them a nutritious snack option. Feel free to customize the seasonings by adding your favorite herbs and spices, such as cumin, paprika, or chili powder, for different flavor variations. Enjoy!

Ants on a log (celery sticks with peanut butter and raisins)

Ingredients:

- Celery stalks
- Peanut butter (or almond butter, sunflower butter, or any other nut or seed butter)
- Raisins (or other dried fruit such as cranberries or chopped dates)

Instructions:

1. Wash the celery stalks thoroughly and cut them into manageable lengths, typically about 3-4 inches long.
2. Spread peanut butter (or your preferred nut or seed butter) onto each celery stick, filling the hollow part of the celery where the strings are.
3. Once the peanut butter is evenly spread on the celery, gently press raisins (or your chosen dried fruit) onto the peanut butter. The raisins will stick to the peanut butter, resembling "ants on a log."
4. Repeat the process for each celery stick until you have made as many as desired.

Ants on a log are a nostalgic and nutritious snack that provides a combination of crunchy celery, creamy nut butter, and sweet raisins. They're perfect for kids and adults alike, whether as an after-school snack, a party appetizer, or a quick energy boost during the day. Feel free to get creative and experiment with different nut or seed butters and dried fruits to suit your taste preferences!

Whole grain toast with mashed banana

Ingredients:

- Whole grain bread slices
- Ripe bananas
- Optional toppings: honey, cinnamon, nut butter, chia seeds, or sliced berries

Instructions:

1. Start by toasting the whole grain bread slices until they are golden brown and crispy.
2. While the toast is toasting, peel the ripe bananas and place them in a bowl.
3. Use a fork to mash the bananas until they are smooth and creamy. You can leave them slightly chunky if you prefer.
4. Once the toast is done, spread a generous layer of mashed banana onto each slice of toast.
5. If desired, drizzle a little honey over the mashed banana for added sweetness.
6. Optional: Sprinkle cinnamon on top of the mashed banana for extra flavor.
7. You can also spread nut butter on the toast before adding the mashed banana for added protein and flavor.
8. Serve the whole grain toast with mashed banana immediately, and enjoy!

This simple yet satisfying snack is packed with fiber, vitamins, and minerals from the whole grain toast and bananas. It's perfect for breakfast, brunch, or a quick and nutritious snack any time of the day. Feel free to customize the toppings with your favorite ingredients to suit your taste preferences.

Frozen grapes

Ingredients:

- Fresh grapes (any variety)
- Optional: lemon juice or flavored extracts for extra flavor

Instructions:

1. Start by washing the grapes thoroughly under cold water.
2. Remove the grapes from the stems and place them in a colander to drain.
3. Once the grapes are washed and drained, spread them out in a single layer on a baking sheet lined with parchment paper or wax paper.
4. If desired, you can sprinkle the grapes with a little lemon juice for a touch of acidity or add a few drops of flavored extracts for extra flavor. This step is optional but can enhance the taste of the frozen grapes.
5. Place the baking sheet with the grapes in the freezer and let them freeze for at least 2-3 hours, or until they are completely frozen.
6. Once the grapes are frozen, remove them from the freezer and transfer them to an airtight container or freezer bag for storage.
7. Keep the frozen grapes in the freezer until ready to serve.

Frozen grapes are a delicious and healthy snack that's perfect for satisfying your sweet tooth. They're naturally sweet, low in calories, and packed with vitamins and antioxidants. Enjoy them straight out of the freezer as a refreshing treat or use them as a tasty addition to smoothies, fruit salads, or yogurt parfaits.

Mini bell peppers filled with hummus

Ingredients:

- Mini bell peppers (any color)
- Hummus (store-bought or homemade)
- Optional toppings: chopped fresh herbs (such as parsley or chives), paprika, sesame seeds, or a drizzle of olive oil

Instructions:

1. Start by washing the mini bell peppers thoroughly and cutting them in half lengthwise.
2. Remove the seeds and membranes from the inside of each pepper half, creating small cups to hold the hummus.
3. Spoon a small amount of hummus into each pepper half, filling them to the top.
4. Optional: Sprinkle chopped fresh herbs, paprika, sesame seeds, or a drizzle of olive oil on top of the hummus-filled pepper halves for added flavor and presentation.
5. Arrange the stuffed mini bell peppers on a serving platter and serve immediately, or refrigerate them until ready to serve.

These mini bell peppers filled with hummus are not only delicious but also packed with vitamins, minerals, and fiber. They're perfect for parties, gatherings, or as a healthy snack any time of the day. Feel free to customize the hummus with your favorite ingredients and seasonings, or use different colored bell peppers for a vibrant presentation. Enjoy!

Cottage cheese with sliced peaches

Ingredients:

- Cottage cheese
- Ripe peaches, sliced (you can use fresh or canned peaches)
- Optional: honey, cinnamon, or chopped nuts for extra flavor

Instructions:

1. Start by washing and slicing the peaches, removing the pits if using fresh peaches.
2. Spoon the desired amount of cottage cheese into a serving bowl or plate.
3. Arrange the sliced peaches on top of the cottage cheese.
4. Optional: Drizzle a little honey over the cottage cheese and peaches for added sweetness, or sprinkle some cinnamon for extra flavor.
5. If desired, you can also sprinkle chopped nuts, such as almonds or walnuts, on top for added texture and crunch.
6. Serve the cottage cheese with sliced peaches immediately and enjoy!

This snack or light meal is not only delicious but also provides a good balance of protein from the cottage cheese and vitamins and fiber from the peaches. It's perfect for breakfast, a snack, or even a healthy dessert option. Feel free to adjust the ingredients and toppings according to your taste preferences.

Seaweed snacks

Ingredients:

- Dried seaweed sheets (nori)
- Toasted sesame oil
- Soy sauce or tamari
- Optional: sesame seeds, chili flakes, or other seasonings of your choice

Instructions:

1. Preheat your oven to 275°F (135°C) and line a baking sheet with parchment paper.
2. Lay the dried seaweed sheets flat on the prepared baking sheet.
3. In a small bowl, mix together toasted sesame oil and soy sauce or tamari to create a flavorful seasoning mixture. You can adjust the ratio of sesame oil to soy sauce/tamari according to your taste preferences.
4. Using a pastry brush or your fingers, lightly brush the seaweed sheets with the seasoning mixture, making sure to coat them evenly.
5. If desired, sprinkle sesame seeds, chili flakes, or other seasonings of your choice over the seaweed sheets for extra flavor.
6. Place the baking sheet in the preheated oven and bake the seaweed sheets for about 15-20 minutes, or until they are crisp and slightly golden brown.
7. Once done, remove the baking sheet from the oven and let the seaweed sheets cool completely before serving.
8. Once cooled, break the seaweed sheets into bite-sized pieces and serve as a crunchy snack.

These homemade seaweed snacks are not only delicious but also packed with vitamins, minerals, and antioxidants. They're perfect for munching on straight out of the oven or as a topping for salads, soups, or rice dishes. Feel free to customize the seasonings and toppings to suit your taste preferences. Enjoy!

Quinoa salad with cucumber and lemon dressing

Ingredients:

For the quinoa salad:

- 1 cup quinoa, rinsed
- 2 cups water or vegetable broth
- 1 cucumber, diced
- 1 bell pepper, diced (any color)
- 1/4 cup red onion, finely chopped
- 1/4 cup fresh parsley, chopped
- 1/4 cup fresh mint, chopped (optional)
- Salt and pepper, to taste

For the lemon dressing:

- 1/4 cup olive oil
- Juice of 1-2 lemons (about 1/4 to 1/3 cup)
- 1-2 cloves garlic, minced
- 1 teaspoon Dijon mustard
- Salt and pepper, to taste

Instructions:

1. In a medium saucepan, combine the quinoa and water or vegetable broth. Bring to a boil, then reduce the heat to low, cover, and simmer for 15-20 minutes, or until the quinoa is cooked and the liquid is absorbed. Remove from heat and let it cool slightly.
2. In a large mixing bowl, combine the cooked quinoa, diced cucumber, diced bell pepper, chopped red onion, chopped parsley, and chopped mint (if using). Season with salt and pepper to taste.
3. In a small bowl or jar, whisk together the olive oil, lemon juice, minced garlic, Dijon mustard, salt, and pepper to make the lemon dressing.

4. Pour the lemon dressing over the quinoa salad and toss until everything is well coated.
5. Taste and adjust the seasoning if needed.
6. Serve the quinoa salad immediately, or chill it in the refrigerator for at least 30 minutes to allow the flavors to meld together.
7. Before serving, give the salad a final toss and garnish with additional fresh herbs, if desired.

This quinoa salad with cucumber and lemon dressing is light, flavorful, and packed with protein, fiber, and vitamins. It's perfect for meal prep, picnics, potlucks, or as a healthy side dish for any occasion. Enjoy!

Rice crackers with avocado and smoked salmon

Ingredients:

- Rice crackers
- Ripe avocados
- Smoked salmon slices
- Optional toppings: lemon juice, black pepper, fresh dill, capers, or microgreens

Instructions:

1. Start by slicing the avocados and removing the pits. Scoop out the flesh into a bowl and mash it with a fork until smooth or slightly chunky, according to your preference.
2. If desired, season the mashed avocado with a squeeze of lemon juice and a sprinkle of black pepper for extra flavor.
3. Spread a generous layer of mashed avocado onto each rice cracker.
4. Next, place a slice of smoked salmon on top of the mashed avocado layer on each rice cracker.
5. If desired, garnish each rice cracker with additional toppings such as fresh dill, capers, or microgreens for added flavor and presentation.
6. Arrange the rice crackers with avocado and smoked salmon on a serving platter and serve immediately.

These rice crackers with avocado and smoked salmon are not only delicious but also elegant and easy to prepare. They're perfect for entertaining guests, parties, or as a light meal or snack anytime. Feel free to customize the toppings and seasonings according to your taste preferences. Enjoy!

Beet chips

Ingredients:

- Fresh beets
- Olive oil
- Salt and pepper, to taste
- Optional: garlic powder, onion powder, smoked paprika, or other seasonings of your choice

Instructions:

1. Preheat your oven to 350°F (175°C) and line a baking sheet with parchment paper or a silicone baking mat.
2. Wash and peel the beets, then slice them thinly using a sharp knife or a mandoline slicer. Aim for uniform slices to ensure even baking.
3. In a large mixing bowl, toss the beet slices with olive oil until they are evenly coated. You want a thin, even layer of oil on each slice to help them crisp up in the oven.
4. Season the beet slices with salt, pepper, and any other seasonings of your choice. Garlic powder, onion powder, and smoked paprika are popular options, but feel free to get creative with your seasonings.
5. Arrange the seasoned beet slices in a single layer on the prepared baking sheet, making sure they are not overlapping.
6. Bake the beet chips in the preheated oven for 20-25 minutes, flipping them halfway through the cooking time, or until they are crisp and golden brown around the edges.
7. Once done, remove the baking sheet from the oven and let the beet chips cool on the pan for a few minutes. They will continue to crisp up as they cool.
8. Transfer the beet chips to a serving bowl or plate and serve them immediately, or let them cool completely before storing them in an airtight container for later use.

These homemade beet chips are not only delicious but also packed with fiber, vitamins, and minerals. They make a nutritious and satisfying snack that's perfect for munching on anytime. Enjoy!

Greek yogurt with chia seeds and honey

Ingredients:

- Greek yogurt (plain or flavored)
- Chia seeds
- Honey (or maple syrup, agave nectar, or your preferred sweetener)

Instructions:

1. In a serving bowl or glass, spoon the desired amount of Greek yogurt.
2. Sprinkle chia seeds on top of the Greek yogurt. You can add as much or as little as you like, depending on your preference.
3. Drizzle honey over the Greek yogurt and chia seeds. The amount of honey can also be adjusted to suit your taste.
4. Optional: Stir the mixture gently to combine the yogurt, chia seeds, and honey evenly.
5. Let the Greek yogurt with chia seeds and honey sit for a few minutes to allow the chia seeds to soften and absorb some of the yogurt.
6. Enjoy the Greek yogurt with chia seeds and honey as a satisfying and nutritious snack or breakfast option!

This simple and wholesome snack is packed with protein, fiber, and omega-3 fatty acids from the Greek yogurt and chia seeds. The honey adds a touch of sweetness, making it a delicious treat that's perfect for any time of day. Feel free to customize the recipe by adding fresh fruit, nuts, or granola for extra flavor and texture.

Caprese skewers (cherry tomatoes, mozzarella balls, and basil)

Ingredients:

- Cherry tomatoes
- Fresh mozzarella balls (also known as bocconcini or ciliegine)
- Fresh basil leaves
- Balsamic glaze (optional, for drizzling)
- Wooden skewers

Instructions:

1. Wash the cherry tomatoes and pat them dry with a paper towel. Rinse the fresh basil leaves as well and set aside.
2. Thread one cherry tomato onto a wooden skewer, followed by a mozzarella ball and then a basil leaf. Repeat this pattern until the skewer is filled, leaving a little space at the top for easy handling.
3. Continue threading the remaining cherry tomatoes, mozzarella balls, and basil leaves onto the skewers until you have made as many skewers as desired.
4. Arrange the Caprese skewers on a serving platter or plate.
5. Optional: Just before serving, drizzle the skewers with balsamic glaze for extra flavor and presentation.
6. Serve the Caprese skewers immediately and enjoy!

These Caprese skewers are not only delicious but also visually appealing, making them a perfect appetizer for parties, gatherings, or any occasion. The combination of sweet cherry tomatoes, creamy mozzarella, and fragrant basil is sure to please everyone's palate. Feel free to customize the recipe by adding a sprinkle of salt, pepper, or dried herbs for extra flavor.

Almond butter and banana roll-ups

Ingredients:

- Whole grain tortillas or wraps
- Almond butter (or your preferred nut or seed butter)
- Ripe bananas
- Optional toppings: honey, cinnamon, shredded coconut, chia seeds, or chopped nuts

Instructions:

1. Start by spreading a layer of almond butter evenly onto a whole grain tortilla or wrap, leaving a small border around the edges.
2. Peel the ripe bananas and place them on top of the almond butter layer, either whole or sliced lengthwise.
3. If desired, drizzle a little honey over the bananas for added sweetness, or sprinkle cinnamon, shredded coconut, chia seeds, or chopped nuts on top for extra flavor and texture.
4. Carefully roll up the tortilla or wrap tightly around the bananas, starting from one edge and rolling towards the other edge.
5. Once rolled up, slice the almond butter and banana roll-up into bite-sized pieces or leave it whole for a larger snack or meal.
6. Repeat the process with the remaining tortillas, almond butter, and bananas until you have made as many roll-ups as desired.
7. Serve the almond butter and banana roll-ups immediately, or wrap them in plastic wrap or foil for later enjoyment.

These almond butter and banana roll-ups are not only tasty but also packed with protein, fiber, and healthy fats, making them a satisfying and nutritious snack or meal option. They're perfect for breakfast on the go, a quick and easy lunch, or a satisfying afternoon pick-me-up. Feel free to customize the recipe with your favorite nut or seed butter and toppings to suit your taste preferences. Enjoy!

Veggie sushi rolls with low-sodium soy sauce

Ingredients for Veggie Sushi Rolls:

- Sushi rice (short-grain rice)
- Nori sheets (seaweed sheets)
- Assorted vegetables for filling (such as cucumber, avocado, carrot, bell pepper, and/or tofu)
- Bamboo sushi rolling mat
- Water (for sealing the rolls)
- Optional: pickled ginger, wasabi, and sesame seeds for serving

Instructions for Veggie Sushi Rolls:

1. Cook the sushi rice according to the package instructions and let it cool to room temperature. Season the rice with a mixture of rice vinegar, sugar, and salt for authentic sushi rice flavor.
2. While the rice is cooling, prepare the vegetables for the filling. Slice them into thin strips or julienne cuts for easy rolling.
3. Place a sheet of nori shiny side down on the bamboo sushi rolling mat.
4. Spread a thin layer of sushi rice evenly over the nori, leaving a small border along the top edge.
5. Arrange the vegetable strips or other fillings horizontally across the rice, slightly below the center of the nori sheet.
6. Using the bamboo sushi rolling mat, carefully roll the sushi away from you, using gentle pressure to compact the ingredients into a tight cylinder. Roll until the edge of the nori reaches the end and seals.
7. Use a sharp knife to slice the sushi roll into individual pieces, wiping the knife with a damp cloth between cuts to prevent sticking.
8. Serve the veggie sushi rolls with low-sodium soy sauce, pickled ginger, wasabi, and sesame seeds on the side for dipping and garnishing.

Ingredients for Low-Sodium Soy Sauce Dip:

- Low-sodium soy sauce
- Optional: a splash of rice vinegar or mirin (Japanese sweet rice wine)

Instructions for Low-Sodium Soy Sauce Dip:

1. In a small dipping bowl, pour low-sodium soy sauce.
2. If desired, add a splash of rice vinegar or mirin for extra flavor. Mix well.
3. Serve the low-sodium soy sauce dip alongside the veggie sushi rolls for dipping.

Enjoy your homemade veggie sushi rolls with low-sodium soy sauce for a delicious and healthy Japanese-inspired meal or snack!

Whole grain pretzels with mustard for dipping

Ingredients:

- Whole grain pretzels
- Mustard (Dijon mustard, yellow mustard, or your favorite variety)

Instructions:

1. Pour mustard into a small dipping bowl or ramekin, placing it in the center of a serving plate or platter.
2. Arrange whole grain pretzels around the dipping bowl, leaving space for easy access.
3. Serve the pretzels with mustard immediately, allowing guests to dip the pretzels into the mustard as desired.
4. Enjoy the whole grain pretzels with mustard as a flavorful and satisfying snack or appetizer!

This snack is not only delicious but also provides a good balance of carbohydrates, protein, and fiber from the whole grain pretzels. Mustard adds a tangy and zesty flavor that complements the salty pretzels perfectly. Feel free to use your favorite type of mustard or experiment with different flavors for dipping. Enjoy!

Baked apple chips

Ingredients:

- Apples (any variety you prefer)
- Lemon juice (optional, to prevent browning)
- Cinnamon (optional, for flavor)

Instructions:

1. Preheat your oven to 200°F (95°C) and line a baking sheet with parchment paper or a silicone baking mat.
2. Wash and dry the apples thoroughly. If desired, you can peel the apples, but leaving the skins on adds extra fiber and nutrients.
3. Using a sharp knife or a mandoline slicer, slice the apples into thin rounds, about 1/8 to 1/4 inch thick. Try to make the slices as uniform as possible for even baking.
4. If you're concerned about the apples browning, you can toss the slices in a bowl with a little lemon juice before arranging them on the baking sheet. This step is optional but can help preserve the color of the apples.
5. Arrange the apple slices in a single layer on the prepared baking sheet, making sure they are not overlapping.
6. If desired, sprinkle cinnamon over the apple slices for added flavor.
7. Place the baking sheet in the preheated oven and bake the apple slices for 1.5 to 2 hours, or until they are crisp and golden brown, flipping them halfway through the baking time.
8. Once the apple chips are done, remove them from the oven and let them cool completely on the baking sheet. They will continue to crisp up as they cool.
9. Once cooled, transfer the baked apple chips to an airtight container or enjoy them immediately as a healthy and satisfying snack!

These homemade baked apple chips are crispy, sweet, and naturally delicious. They're perfect for munching on anytime you're craving a crunchy snack, and they're much healthier than store-bought chips since they contain no added sugars or preservatives. Experiment with different apple varieties and flavorings to find your favorite combination. Enjoy!

Guacamole with cucumber slices

Ingredients for Guacamole:

- 2 ripe avocados
- 1 small tomato, diced
- 1/4 cup red onion, finely chopped
- 1/4 cup cilantro, chopped
- 1 lime, juiced
- Salt and pepper, to taste
- Optional: jalapeño or serrano pepper, finely chopped (for extra heat)

Ingredients for Cucumber Slices:

- 1 English cucumber, washed and sliced

Instructions:

1. Start by preparing the guacamole. Cut the avocados in half, remove the pits, and scoop the flesh into a mixing bowl.
2. Mash the avocado with a fork until smooth or slightly chunky, depending on your preference.
3. Add the diced tomato, chopped red onion, chopped cilantro, and lime juice to the mashed avocado. Mix until well combined.
4. Season the guacamole with salt and pepper to taste. If you like your guacamole spicy, you can also add finely chopped jalapeño or serrano pepper at this point.
5. Cover the guacamole with plastic wrap, pressing it down onto the surface to prevent browning, and refrigerate for at least 30 minutes to allow the flavors to meld together.
6. While the guacamole is chilling, prepare the cucumber slices. Wash the cucumber thoroughly, then slice it into thin rounds using a sharp knife or a mandoline slicer.
7. Once the guacamole is chilled and the cucumber slices are ready, arrange the cucumber slices on a serving platter or plate.
8. Serve the chilled guacamole alongside the cucumber slices for dipping or spreading.

9. Enjoy the guacamole with cucumber slices as a healthy and delicious snack or appetizer!

This combination is not only tasty but also provides a good balance of healthy fats, vitamins, and minerals. The cool and crisp cucumber slices complement the creamy and flavorful guacamole perfectly. Feel free to adjust the seasonings and add-ins to suit your taste preferences. Enjoy!

Brown rice cakes with almond butter and sliced strawberries

Ingredients:

- Brown rice cakes
- Almond butter (or your preferred nut or seed butter)
- Fresh strawberries, washed and sliced

Instructions:

1. Spread a generous layer of almond butter onto each brown rice cake, covering the entire surface.
2. Place a few slices of fresh strawberries on top of the almond butter layer, arranging them evenly.
3. Optional: Drizzle a little honey or sprinkle some cinnamon on top for extra sweetness and flavor.
4. Serve the brown rice cakes with almond butter and sliced strawberries immediately and enjoy!

These rice cakes with almond butter and strawberries are not only delicious but also packed with fiber, protein, and vitamins. They make a satisfying and wholesome snack or light meal that's perfect for any time of day. Feel free to customize the toppings with your favorite fruits, such as bananas or raspberries, or add a sprinkle of chia seeds or shredded coconut for extra texture. Enjoy!

Greek yogurt dip with fresh vegetables

Ingredients for Greek Yogurt Dip:

- 1 cup Greek yogurt (plain or flavored)
- 1 tablespoon olive oil
- 1 tablespoon lemon juice
- 1 clove garlic, minced
- 1 tablespoon chopped fresh herbs (such as dill, parsley, or chives)
- Salt and pepper, to taste

Ingredients for Fresh Vegetables:

- Assorted fresh vegetables for dipping (such as carrots, cucumber, bell peppers, cherry tomatoes, celery, and broccoli)

Instructions:

1. In a mixing bowl, combine the Greek yogurt, olive oil, lemon juice, minced garlic, chopped fresh herbs, salt, and pepper. Stir until well combined.
2. Taste the Greek yogurt dip and adjust the seasoning if needed, adding more salt, pepper, or lemon juice according to your taste preferences.
3. Transfer the Greek yogurt dip to a serving bowl and garnish with additional chopped herbs, if desired.
4. Wash and prepare the fresh vegetables for dipping. Cut them into bite-sized pieces or sticks for easy dipping.
5. Arrange the prepared fresh vegetables on a serving platter or tray around the bowl of Greek yogurt dip.
6. Serve the Greek yogurt dip with fresh vegetables immediately and enjoy!

This Greek yogurt dip is creamy, tangy, and packed with flavor, while the fresh vegetables add crunch, color, and nutrition. It's a perfect snack or appetizer for parties, gatherings, or anytime you're craving a healthy and satisfying treat. Feel free to customize the dip with your favorite herbs and spices, or add a pinch of cayenne pepper or paprika for extra heat. Enjoy dipping!

Cottage cheese with sliced kiwi

Ingredients:

- Cottage cheese
- Ripe kiwi fruit, peeled and sliced

Instructions:

1. Spoon cottage cheese into a serving bowl or plate, depending on your preference.
2. Wash and peel the kiwi fruit, then slice it into rounds or wedges.
3. Arrange the sliced kiwi on top of the cottage cheese, either scattered or neatly arranged.
4. Optional: For added sweetness, you can drizzle a little honey or maple syrup over the cottage cheese and kiwi slices.
5. Serve the cottage cheese with sliced kiwi immediately and enjoy!

This snack is not only delicious but also provides a good balance of protein, fiber, vitamins, and minerals. The creamy texture of the cottage cheese pairs well with the tartness of the kiwi fruit, creating a delightful combination of flavors and textures. Enjoy it as a quick and nutritious snack, a light breakfast, or a refreshing dessert!

Veggie sticks with homemade ranch dip

Ingredients for Homemade Ranch Dip:

- 1 cup plain Greek yogurt
- 1/4 cup mayonnaise
- 1 tablespoon lemon juice
- 1 teaspoon Dijon mustard
- 1 clove garlic, minced
- 1 teaspoon onion powder
- 1 teaspoon dried dill
- 1 teaspoon dried parsley
- Salt and pepper, to taste

Ingredients for Veggie Sticks:

- Assorted fresh vegetables for dipping (such as carrots, celery, bell peppers, cucumber, and cherry tomatoes), washed and cut into sticks or slices

Instructions:

1. In a mixing bowl, combine the plain Greek yogurt, mayonnaise, lemon juice, Dijon mustard, minced garlic, onion powder, dried dill, dried parsley, salt, and pepper. Stir until well combined.
2. Taste the ranch dip and adjust the seasoning if needed, adding more salt, pepper, lemon juice, or herbs according to your taste preferences.
3. Transfer the homemade ranch dip to a serving bowl and garnish with a sprinkle of dried herbs, if desired.
4. Arrange the prepared fresh vegetables on a serving platter or tray alongside the bowl of ranch dip.
5. Serve the veggie sticks with homemade ranch dip immediately and enjoy!

This homemade ranch dip is creamy, flavorful, and packed with herbs and spices, while the fresh vegetables add crunch, color, and nutrition. It's a perfect snack or appetizer for parties, gatherings, or anytime you're craving a healthy and satisfying treat. Feel free to customize the dip with your favorite herbs and spices, or add a pinch of cayenne pepper or paprika for extra heat. Enjoy dipping!

Peanut butter and jelly on whole grain crackers

Ingredients:

- Whole grain crackers
- Peanut butter (creamy or crunchy)
- Jelly or jam (any flavor you prefer)

Instructions:

1. Take whole grain crackers and spread a layer of peanut butter onto each one. You can use as much or as little peanut butter as you like, depending on your preference.
2. Spoon a dollop of jelly or jam on top of the peanut butter layer on each cracker. Again, adjust the amount based on your taste preferences.
3. Carefully place another whole grain cracker on top of each one to create a sandwich.
4. Repeat the process until you have made as many peanut butter and jelly crackers as desired.
5. Serve the peanut butter and jelly crackers immediately and enjoy!

This snack is not only delicious but also provides a good balance of protein, healthy fats, and carbohydrates from the peanut butter, as well as vitamins and minerals from the whole grain crackers and fruit jelly or jam. It's perfect for a quick energy boost or as a satisfying treat anytime you're craving something sweet and savory. Feel free to experiment with different flavors of jelly or jam, or add sliced fruit like bananas or strawberries for extra flavor and nutrition. Enjoy!

Baked cinnamon apple slices

Ingredients:

- 3-4 medium-sized apples (any variety you prefer)
- 1-2 tablespoons melted butter or coconut oil
- 1-2 tablespoons honey or maple syrup (optional, for added sweetness)
- 1 teaspoon ground cinnamon
- Pinch of ground nutmeg (optional)
- Pinch of ground cloves (optional)

Instructions:

1. Preheat your oven to 350°F (175°C) and line a baking sheet with parchment paper or a silicone baking mat.
2. Wash the apples thoroughly and core them using an apple corer or a knife. You can peel the apples if you prefer, but leaving the skins on adds extra fiber and nutrients.
3. Slice the cored apples into thin rounds using a sharp knife or a mandoline slicer. Aim for slices that are about 1/4 inch thick.
4. In a large mixing bowl, combine the melted butter or coconut oil with the honey or maple syrup (if using). Add the ground cinnamon, and if desired, the ground nutmeg and ground cloves. Stir until well combined.
5. Add the apple slices to the bowl with the cinnamon mixture and toss until the slices are evenly coated.
6. Arrange the coated apple slices in a single layer on the prepared baking sheet, making sure they are not overlapping.
7. Bake the apple slices in the preheated oven for 20-25 minutes, or until they are tender and lightly golden brown around the edges. You can flip the slices halfway through the baking time for more even cooking.
8. Once the apple slices are done, remove them from the oven and let them cool slightly before serving.
9. Serve the baked cinnamon apple slices warm as a snack, dessert, or topping for oatmeal, yogurt, or ice cream.

These baked cinnamon apple slices are naturally sweet and fragrant, with warm spices adding a cozy touch. They're a healthier alternative to store-bought snacks and are perfect for satisfying your sweet tooth without any guilt. Enjoy!

Whole grain pita chips with roasted red pepper hummus

Ingredients for Whole Grain Pita Chips:

- Whole grain pita bread
- Olive oil
- Salt
- Optional: garlic powder, paprika, or other seasonings of your choice

Ingredients for Roasted Red Pepper Hummus:

- 1 can (15 ounces) chickpeas, drained and rinsed
- 1/4 cup tahini
- 1/4 cup lemon juice
- 2 tablespoons olive oil
- 2 cloves garlic, minced
- 1/2 teaspoon ground cumin
- 1/2 teaspoon salt
- 1/4 cup jarred roasted red peppers, drained
- 2-3 tablespoons water (optional, for desired consistency)

Instructions for Whole Grain Pita Chips:

1. Preheat your oven to 375°F (190°C) and line a baking sheet with parchment paper or a silicone baking mat.
2. Cut the whole grain pita bread into wedges or triangles.
3. In a small bowl, mix together olive oil, salt, and any optional seasonings you like.
4. Brush both sides of the pita wedges with the olive oil mixture.
5. Place the pita wedges in a single layer on the prepared baking sheet.
6. Bake in the preheated oven for 10-12 minutes, flipping halfway through, or until the pita chips are golden and crispy.
7. Remove from the oven and let cool slightly before serving.

Instructions for Roasted Red Pepper Hummus:

1. In a food processor, combine the chickpeas, tahini, lemon juice, olive oil, minced garlic, ground cumin, and salt.
2. Add the roasted red peppers to the food processor.
3. Blend until smooth, scraping down the sides of the bowl as needed. If the hummus is too thick, you can add water, 1 tablespoon at a time, until you reach your desired consistency.
4. Taste the hummus and adjust the seasoning if needed, adding more lemon juice, salt, or cumin to taste.
5. Transfer the roasted red pepper hummus to a serving bowl.
6. Serve the whole grain pita chips with the roasted red pepper hummus and enjoy!

These whole grain pita chips with roasted red pepper hummus are flavorful, crunchy, and nutritious. They're perfect for snacking, parties, or as an appetizer before a meal. Feel free to customize the seasonings and adjust the consistency of the hummus to suit your taste preferences. Enjoy!

Low-sodium turkey roll-ups with lettuce and mustard

Ingredients:

- Low-sodium turkey slices
- Lettuce leaves (such as romaine or butter lettuce)
- Mustard (Dijon, yellow, or your preferred variety)

Instructions:

1. Lay out a slice of low-sodium turkey on a clean work surface, such as a cutting board.
2. Place a lettuce leaf on top of the turkey slice, covering it completely.
3. Spread a thin layer of mustard evenly over the lettuce leaf. Use as much or as little mustard as you like, depending on your taste preferences.
4. Starting from one end, tightly roll up the turkey slice with the lettuce and mustard inside. Continue rolling until you reach the other end.
5. If desired, you can secure the roll-up with a toothpick to help keep it together.
6. Repeat the process with the remaining turkey slices, lettuce leaves, and mustard until you have made as many roll-ups as desired.
7. Serve the low-sodium turkey roll-ups with lettuce and mustard immediately, or refrigerate them for later enjoyment.

These turkey roll-ups are not only tasty but also low in sodium, making them a healthy option for those watching their salt intake. They're packed with protein, fiber, and vitamins from the turkey and lettuce, and the mustard adds a tangy kick without adding extra sodium. Enjoy them as a satisfying snack, light lunch, or appetizer anytime you're craving a nutritious and flavorful bite!

Mixed nuts (unsalted)

Ingredients:

- Mixed nuts (such as almonds, walnuts, cashews, pecans, and peanuts)

Instructions:

1. Purchase a variety of unsalted mixed nuts from your local grocery store or bulk food store. You can choose your favorite nuts or try a pre-packaged mix for convenience.
2. If the nuts are not already shelled, you may need to shell them before enjoying. Alternatively, you can purchase pre-shelled nuts for convenience.
3. Place a handful of mixed nuts in a small bowl or snack container for easy portion control.
4. Enjoy the mixed nuts as a snack on their own, or incorporate them into other dishes such as salads, oatmeal, yogurt, or baked goods.
5. Store any remaining mixed nuts in an airtight container in a cool, dry place to maintain freshness.

Mixed nuts are a delicious and satisfying snack that's perfect for curbing hunger between meals or providing a quick energy boost on the go. They're also a great addition to a balanced diet, providing essential nutrients that support overall health and well-being. Enjoy them as part of a healthy lifestyle!

Rice cakes with mashed avocado and sliced hard-boiled eggs

Ingredients:

- Rice cakes
- Ripe avocado
- Hard-boiled eggs
- Salt and pepper, to taste
- Optional toppings: red pepper flakes, chili powder, paprika, or sesame seeds

Instructions:

1. Start by preparing the mashed avocado. Cut the avocado in half, remove the pit, and scoop the flesh into a bowl. Mash the avocado with a fork until smooth or slightly chunky, according to your preference. Season with salt and pepper to taste.
2. Peel the hard-boiled eggs and slice them into rounds or wedges.
3. Place a spoonful of mashed avocado onto each rice cake, spreading it evenly to cover the surface.
4. Arrange the sliced hard-boiled eggs on top of the mashed avocado layer, distributing them evenly.
5. Sprinkle with additional salt and pepper, if desired, and add any optional toppings such as red pepper flakes, chili powder, paprika, or sesame seeds for extra flavor and texture.
6. Serve the rice cakes with mashed avocado and sliced hard-boiled eggs immediately, or store them in the refrigerator for later enjoyment.

These rice cakes with mashed avocado and sliced hard-boiled eggs are not only delicious but also packed with protein, healthy fats, and fiber, making them a nutritious and satisfying snack or light meal option. Feel free to customize the toppings and seasonings according to your taste preferences. Enjoy!

Baked carrot fries

Ingredients:

- Carrots (about 4-5 medium-sized)
- Olive oil
- Salt and pepper, to taste
- Optional seasonings: garlic powder, paprika, cumin, or your favorite herbs and spices

Instructions:

1. Preheat your oven to 425°F (220°C) and line a baking sheet with parchment paper or aluminum foil for easy cleanup.
2. Wash and peel the carrots, then cut them into thin strips resembling fries. Try to make the strips as uniform as possible for even cooking.
3. Place the carrot strips in a mixing bowl and drizzle with olive oil, tossing to coat evenly. You want a light, even coating of oil on all the carrot strips.
4. Season the carrot strips with salt, pepper, and any optional seasonings of your choice. Toss again to ensure the seasonings are evenly distributed.
5. Arrange the seasoned carrot strips in a single layer on the prepared baking sheet, making sure they are not overlapping.
6. Bake the carrot fries in the preheated oven for 20-25 minutes, flipping them halfway through the cooking time, or until they are golden brown and crispy on the outside.
7. Once done, remove the baking sheet from the oven and let the carrot fries cool for a few minutes before serving.
8. Serve the baked carrot fries hot with your favorite dipping sauce, such as ketchup, ranch dressing, or aioli.

These baked carrot fries are a tasty and nutritious snack or side dish that's packed with vitamins, minerals, and fiber. They're crispy on the outside and tender on the inside, making them a satisfying alternative to traditional fries. Feel free to experiment with different seasonings and dipping sauces to suit your taste preferences. Enjoy!

Greek yogurt with mango chunks

Ingredients:

- Greek yogurt (plain or flavored)
- Ripe mango, peeled and diced into chunks

Instructions:

1. Spoon Greek yogurt into a serving bowl or glass, depending on your preference.
2. Wash, peel, and dice a ripe mango into bite-sized chunks.
3. Add the diced mango chunks on top of the Greek yogurt.
4. Optional: If desired, you can drizzle a little honey or maple syrup over the Greek yogurt and mango chunks for added sweetness.
5. Serve the Greek yogurt with mango chunks immediately and enjoy!

This simple and refreshing snack is packed with protein, probiotics, vitamins, and minerals from the Greek yogurt, while the mango provides natural sweetness, fiber, and antioxidants. It's perfect for breakfast, a midday snack, or a healthy dessert option. Feel free to customize the recipe by adding other fruits, such as berries or pineapple, or topping it with nuts, seeds, or granola for extra flavor and texture. Enjoy!

www.ingramcontent.com/pod-product-compliance
Lightning Source LLC
LaVergne TN
LVHW061948070526
838199LV00060B/4027